Classifying Mammals

www.heinemann.co.uk/library
Visit our website to find out more information about **Heinemann Library** books.

To order:
☎ Phone 44 (0) 1865 888066
▤ Send a fax to 44 (0) 1865 314091
💻 Visit the Heinemann Bookshop at www.heinemann.co.uk/library to browse our catalogue and order online.

First published in Great Britain by Heinemann Library, Halley Court, Jordan Hill, Oxford OX2 8EJ, a division of Harcourt Education Ltd. Heinemann is a registered trademark of Harcourt Education Ltd.

Editorial: Jilly Attwood and Jennifer Tubbs
Design: Jo Hinton-Malivoire and AMR
Illustrations: David Woodroffe
...rine Bevan, Hannah

British Library Cataloguing in Publication Data
Solway, Andrew
Classifying Living Things – Mammals
599'.012
A full catalogue record for this book is available from the British Library.

Acknowledgements
For Harriet, Eliza and Nicholas

The publishers would like to thank the following for permission to reproduce photographs: Bruce Coleman: **11** (John Cancalosi), **23** (Jorg and Petra Wegner), **25** (Jorg and Petra Wegner), **26** (Gunter Kohler), **29** (Alain Compost); Corbis: **12,13** (Roger Tidman); Digital Stock: **5, 20**; Digital Vision: **21**; Harcourt Index: **28**; Natural History Museum: **7**; Nature Picture Library: **4** (Richard du Toit), **6** (Hanne and Jens Eriksen), **9** (Staffan Widstrand), **18** (Francois Savigny), **19** (Dan Burton); **22** (Pete Oxford), **24** (Staffan Widstrand); Oxford Scientific Films: **15**, **10** (E.R.Degginner), **14** (Mary Plage), **17** (Paul Franklin), **16** (Tim Shepherd); RSPCA: **27**.

Cover photograph of zebras at a watering hole reproduced with permission of Nature ...Library.

...uld like to thank Catherine ...ducator, for her ...n of this book.

...ct
...duced
...d in

Contents

Words in the text in bold, **like this**, are explained in the Glossary.

The variety of life

Think of an animal – the first one that comes into your head. The chances are that the animal you think of is a mammal. Pets such as cats and dogs, most of our farm animals, lions, zebras, elephants, mice, dolphins and of course humans – all these and more are mammals. Wherever you look around the world, most of the large animals are mammals.

Scientists can identify thousands of different kinds, or **species** of mammal, ranging from tiny pygmy shrews to huge blue whales. To try and understand how all these different animals are related to each other, scientists classify them – they sort them into groups.

Sorting the living world

When you sort things, it makes them easier to think about and understand. Scientists try to classify living things in a way that tells you how closely one group of animals or plants is related to another. To do this, they compare groups of living things with each other. They look at everything about a living thing, from its colour and shape to the **genes** inside its **cells**. They also look at **fossils**, which give them clues about how living things have changed over time. Then they use all this information to sort the millions of different living things into groups.

Mammals come in all shapes and sizes.

A species is a single kind of animal or plant, such as a mouse or a buttercup. Species that are very similar to each other (for instance, different species of mice) are put together in a larger group called a **genus** (plural genera). Genera that are similar to each other are grouped into **families**, and similar families make up larger groups called **orders**. Closely related orders are grouped into **classes**, classes are grouped into **phyla** (singular phylum), and finally, phyla are grouped into huge groups called kingdoms. Plants, for example, are all in one kingdom, while animals are in another.

Scientific names

Many living things have a common name. But when scientists classify living things, they give every species a two-part scientific name, which is the same the world over. The first part of the scientific name tells you the genus that the creature belongs to. The second part of the name tells you the species within that genus. Leopards, for instance, have the scientific name *Panthera pardus*.

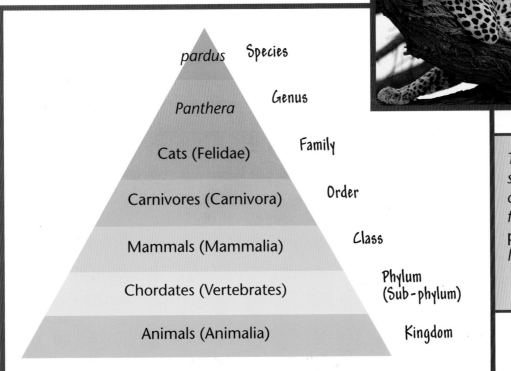

pardus	Species
Panthera	Genus
Cats (Felidae)	Family
Carnivores (Carnivora)	Order
Mammals (Mammalia)	Class
Chordates (Vertebrates)	Phylum (Sub-phylum)
Animals (Animalia)	Kingdom

This diagram shows the full classification for Panthera pardus – a leopard.

Furry milk-drinkers

Within the animal kingdom, mammals are part of a group called the vertebrates. If you feel down the middle of your back, you can feel the bones of your spine, or backbone. These bones are called vertebrae. So vertebrates are animals with backbones. Amphibians, reptiles, birds and mammals are all vertebrates.

What is a mammal?

Mammals have features in common, which separate them from the other groups of vertebrates. Birds have feathers, reptiles are scaly, but mammals are usually hairy or furry. A few, such as humans and whales, have lost much of their hair, but they do have some hair at some point in their lives.

Birds, reptiles and amphibians all lay eggs, but mammals give birth to live babies. Two very unusual types of mammal, the platypuses and the echidnas, do however lay eggs.

Mammals are **warm-blooded**. This means that their bodies stay at one temperature, whatever the temperature around them. All mammal mothers feed their young on milk made in their **mammary glands**. This is why they are called mammals.

*Mammal milk is full of **nutrients**. Mammal babies like this camel grow quickly on this rich food.*

The first mammals

Around 248 million years ago, even before the first dinosaurs appeared, a great extinction took place across the Earth. More than 90 per cent of all animal **species** died out. Many new types of animals appeared after this extinction. These included dinosaurs and the earliest mammals.

The early mammals were small insect-eaters like today's shrews. For millions of years they remained small, while the dinosaurs became the most successful large animals.

Then about 65 million years ago, another great extinction wiped out the dinosaurs. But mammals survived, and many new species appeared because there was no longer competition for food and space from the dinosaurs.

Evolving and adapting

Over thousands or millions of years, groups of living things may evolve (change) so that they are better **adapted** to their habitat (the place they live). This happens because living things that are better adapted live longer and produce more offspring. All the mammals we see today have evolved from a single group of **ancestors**.

Early mammals probably looked like this Morganucodon. This is a reconstruction of a mammal that lived during the Jurassic period.

Mammal orders

There are about 4600 **species** of mammals. They are grouped into 21 different **orders**.

The orders are shown in the table below.

Order	No. of species	Examples
Egg-laying mammals Monotremata (monotremes)	3	platypuses, echidnas
Pouched animals Marsupialia (marsupials)	272	kangaroos, wombats, koalas, opossums
Placental mammals Rodentia (rodents)	over 2,000	mice, rats, squirrels, voles, hamsters, beavers, porcupines
Chiroptera	925	bats
Insectivora (Insectivores)	375	shrews, moles, hedgehogs
Carnivora (Carnivores)	235	cats, dogs, wolves, foxes, badgers, weasels, stoats, mongooses, otters
Primates	233	lemurs, monkeys, apes, humans
Artiodactyla (artiodactyls)	220	sheep, cattle, pigs, goats, deer, antelopes, pigs, giraffes
Lagomorpha	80	rabbits, hares
Cetacea	79	whales, dolphins, porpoises
Pinnipedia	35	seals, walruses, sea lions
Xenarthra (edentates)	29	anteaters, armadillos, sloths
Dermoptera	2	colugos (flying lemurs)
Macroscelidea	19	elephant shrews
Scandentia	19	tree shrews
Perissodactyla	18	horses, zebras, donkeys, rhinos, tapirs
Pholidota	7	pangolins
Hyracoidea	7	hyraxes
Sirenia	4	manatees, dugongs
Proboscidea	2	elephants
Tubulidentata	1	aardvark

Sometimes it is hard to see why a group of species all belong to the same order. Weasels and polar bears, for example, don't look very similar, but are both members of the order Carnivora (Carnivores). They are linked by the long teeth in their upper and lower jaws, which work together like a pair of scissors to slice through flesh.

Eggs and pouches

Most mammals give birth to live young. While the babies grow inside their mothers, they get food from a special **organ** called the placenta. They are called **placental mammals**.

But in two mammal orders, the monotremes and the **marsupials**, things are different. Monotremes are very unusual mammals that lay eggs. There are only three monotreme species: two types of echidna and the duck-billed platypus. They are found in Australia and New Guinea. Monotremes count as mammals because they are furry and **warm-blooded**, and because baby platypuses and echidnas feed on milk from their mother's **mammary glands**.

Marsupials, such as kangaroos and koalas, give birth to live young, but the newborn babies are extremely tiny and helpless. They spend their first weeks of life in the safety of their mother's pouch.

Echidnas are a little like hedgehogs, because their coat has spines as well as hairs. They eat ants and termites, which they lick up with their long, sticky tongues.

Pouched mammals

Marsupials are named after the pouch (marsupium) that they carry their babies around in. They have this pouch because the young are still very tiny and helpless when they are born and need to be protected from **predators**. Koalas, kangaroos, wombats, bandicoots, possums, opossums and the Tasmanian devil are all familiar marsupials. Most marsupials live in Australia, but there are also marsupials in South America and one **species** in North America.

Plugging in to mum

Marsupial babies are born no bigger than honeybees. The only part that is well developed is one front claw. They use this claw to drag themselves from the birth canal to their mother's pouch. There, each baby fastens itself on to a teat, and begins to drink milk. The teat swells in the baby's mouth, so the baby is firmly 'plugged in' to its mother.

Marsupial young suckle for four to five weeks before they begin to leave the pouch. At first they leave the pouch only for a short time, but gradually they become independent.

Kangaroos produce only one baby at a time, but this opossum can produce as many as 25 babies. However, an opossum mother has only 13 teats, so some of the babies do not survive.

A few of the smaller marsupials do not have a pouch, but they still produce undeveloped young that attach themselves to their mother's teats.

Tasmanian devils are ferocious marsupial predators that are active mainly at night.

Bigfoot bounders

Kangaroos and wallabies are a **family** of marsupials that all have powerful back legs, large feet and a long, muscular tail. Most of them graze on grass and are active at night. Because of their huge feet, the family is called the Macropodidae, which means 'big feet'.

When it is grazing, a kangaroo moves about on all fours, but when it senses danger it bounds away on its powerful back legs. A kangaroo's leap can take it 3 metres high and 10 metres along. It could clear a couple of cars in one jump.

Possums and opossums

Many marsupial species are known as possums or opossums. Possums are a family of small marsupials found in Australia. Opossums are small marsupials of South and North America.

The brush-tailed possums in Australia and the Virginia opossum in North America have **adapted** well to living alongside humans. This is partly because they are active only at night, and because they eat a wide variety of foods. Virginia opossums are famous for 'playing possum' (pretending to be dead). They do this as a defence against predators.

Chisel-toothed chewers

Mice, rats, voles, hamsters, squirrels, beavers and porcupines are all rodents. Rodents are the biggest mammal **order**, with over 2000 different **species**.

All rodents have long, strong front teeth called incisors, which they use for gnawing (chewing). The front of each incisor has a thin, very hard coating, while the back part of the tooth is a little softer. As a rodent gnaws at its food, the back of the tooth wears away more quickly, leaving the tooth with a razor-sharp edge. Most rodents use their incisors to eat nuts, seeds, leaves and other plant food.

Fast breeders

Small rodents are a tasty bite for all kinds of **predators**. This is one reason why the lives of rodents are often short. Rodents make up for their short lives by producing large numbers of young very quickly. Hamster mothers have up to 12 babies at once, and a lemming mother can produce over 100 babies in 6 months! The babies are tiny, blind and helpless when they are born, but they grow very quickly. A few rodents, such as beavers and the South American cavies, take longer to produce their young.

Flying squirrels have flaps of skin between their front and back legs, which they spread out into 'wings' as they leap from tree to tree. They can glide long distances this way.

Rodent lifestyles

To avoid predators, many rodents rest during the day and feed at night. Many burrow into the ground, making holes and tunnels where they can rest in relative safety. Some, like the blind mole rats, spend their whole lives underground. Lemmings live in cold climates, and in the winter they dig tunnels under the snow instead of tunnelling into the ground.

Some burrowers live alone, but others live in huge colonies. Hundreds of prairie dogs, for instance, live together in enormous underground 'towns'.

Some rodents are tree-dwellers. Many squirrel species live in trees, but there are also tree rats, tree mice and even tree porcupines.

Beavers, water rats, water voles and coypus are all water-living rodents. Beavers and coypus eat only plants, but fish-eating rats are fierce water predators. Beavers are famous for blocking rivers or streams with dams to make lakes, where they build their homes.

Coypus come originally from South America, but people have introduced coypus to Europe and the USA, where they have survived and spread.

Rabbits and hares

Rabbits and hares have large incisor teeth, like rodents. But they also have a second pair of smaller incisors. This and other differences mean that rabbits and hares are not rodents, but are near relatives. They are classified in their own order, the lagomorphs.

Long-fingered fliers

Although birds may rule the air by day, at night bats are masters of the skies. Other mammals such as 'flying' squirrels are good gliders, but bats are the only mammals that have wings and can fly. Unlike birds, which have wings made of feathers, a bat's wings are flaps of skin. The finger bones of the bat's 'hands' have become enormously long to support this skin. The name for the bat **order** is Chiroptera, which means 'hand wing'.

Bats can be divided into two groups, the 'microbats' and the 'megabats'. Microbats are generally smaller, and eat insects, while megabats are larger and eat fruit. But the main difference between the groups is that megabats have super-sensitive night sight, while microbats use sounds to find their way around in the dark.

A group of grey-headed flying foxes roosting. Almost all bats roost upside down, hanging from a branch, or the wall of a cave, or in a hollow tree trunk. In colder countries bats hibernate (sleep through the winter) in this way.

Megabats

Megabats are also known as fruit bats. Their bodies are furry, they have large eyes and a pointed nose. Their faces look like foxes' faces, so some fruit bats are also known as flying foxes. They have a good sense of smell as well as good eyesight, and use their noses to smell out the ripest fruit.

Fruit bats only live in warm, tropical countries, where there is enough fruit for them to eat all year round. During the day fruit bats roost (rest and sleep) in large groups, often hanging from the branches of trees.

Microbats

Microbats are also known as insect-eating bats, because nearly all of them feed on insects. They also often live in groups. When female bats are having babies they gather in colonies of up to 20 million. These colonies usually gather in caves.

Microbats have small eyes, because sight is not an important sense for them. They use sound to find their way around in the dark and to catch flying insects. As they fly, the bats send out a string of short, high squeaks. The squeaks are so high that people cannot hear them. These sounds echo off objects around the bat, and its sensitive ears pick up the returning echoes. The bats can use the echoes to build up an 'echo picture' of the world around them. This is called **echolocation**.

Horseshoe bats make sounds through their nose. The horseshoe shape of the nose concentrates the sounds into a beam. As a bat homes in on an insect its calls get faster and faster, so that it can accurately track the insect.

Insect specialists

An insectivore is an animal that eats mostly insects. Many mammals are insectivores, but there is also an **order** of mammals called the Insectivores. Shrews, moles and hedgehogs are all Insectivores. They eat insects, spiders, worms and other minibeasts.

This pygmy shrew is tiny, but it has a huge appetite. Small animals lose heat very quickly, and must 'burn' lots of food to keep warm. A small shrew must eat over three times its own body weight each day to stay alive.

Anteaters and armadillos are also insect-eaters. They belong to an order called edentates, which means 'toothless'. The sloth is also an edentate, but it only eats plants.

Insectivores

Insectivores are small animals with long, sensitive noses. Most are **nocturnal** (active at night), and live on the ground or in burrows. They rely more on smell and touch than on their small eyes. Some insectivores are thought to be similar to the early **ancestors** of all **placental mammals**.

Three-quarters of Insectivores are shrews – mouse-like creatures with small ears and long noses. They eat insects and other small creatures. Shrews produce a strong smell that puts many **predators** off, and some **species** have a poisonous bite.

Moles have strong front legs and thick claws designed for digging. They dig deep burrows, with a central chamber and rings of tunnels around it. A mole's favourite food is worms, but it also eats insects and other animals.

Instead of fur, hedgehogs have a coat of sharp spines. When an enemy threatens them, they curl up into a prickly ball. In cooler climates, they hibernate (sleep through the winter).

Toothless mammals

The edentates are made up of insect-eating anteaters and armadillos, plus sloths, which are plant-eaters. The three groups look very different, but they are closely related. The bones of their lower back are different from those of all other mammals. Anteaters have no teeth, but armadillos and sloths have small, simple, peg-like teeth. All have long, strong claws on their front feet.

Anteaters live on the ground or in trees. They eat only ants and termites, licking them up with a long, sticky tongue. Giant anteaters use their strong front claws to break open anthills and termite nests.

Armadillos have armour plating, which protects them from predators. In the daytime they sleep in burrows and at night they roam about, using their claws to dig for insects. They can smell insects 20 centimetres below the surface.

Most edentates live in South America, but nine-banded armadillos are found in the southern USA. Nine-banded armadillo mothers usually give birth to quadruplets – four identical armadillo babies.

Hard-toed runners

Hoofed mammals are specialized for running. They have long legs, and hard, horny hooves that protect their feet as they race along. Although they may not run as fast as some mammals, their hooves allow them to run for longer.

There are two different **orders** of hoofed mammals. One group walk on two toes. These are the even-toed hoofed mammals, for example: sheep, cattle, goats, pigs, antelopes, deer, camels, giraffes and hippos. The other group are the odd-toed hoofed mammals. They walk on either three toes or one toe. Horses, zebras, rhinos and tapirs are all odd-toed.

Springboks don't just rely on running to escape from predators. They try to put them off by 'pronking' – doing huge jumps straight up into the air. Scientists think that pronking springboks are saying to predators, 'I'm really fit and strong: don't waste your energy trying to catch me.'

Hoofed mammal lifestyles

Hoofed mammals are all herbivores (plant eaters). Many live in open grassland or desert, where they need to be able to run fast to escape from big cats and other **predators**. Pigs, deer, goats and llamas live in woodlands or mountain areas, where speed is less important.

Male hoofed mammals often have horns, tusks or antlers, which they use as weapons and to impress females. Herds of hoofed mammals often **migrate** as the seasons change. Their babies can walk and run very soon after they are born. Wildebeest, for instance, can stand five minutes after they are born, and within a day can run with the herd.

Tough food

Plant food such as grasses and leaves are tough and do not contain many **nutrients**. Hoofed mammals need a special **digestive system** to break down this food. In odd-toed mammals the second part of the digestive system – the intestines – is where most of the **digestion** happens.

Most even-toed animals are ruminants. This means that they have several stomachs, and eat their food twice. They eat food quickly, and it goes into a big pouch called the rumen. Here, millions of microscopic creatures break down any tough fibres that the animal itself cannot digest. The food then goes back into the animal's mouth, and it chews it again, more slowly. This is called 'chewing the cud'. After the ruminant swallows the food a second time, the food goes into another stomach, where normal digestion begins.

Asian giant

The biggest land mammal ever was a rhino-like hoofed animal called *Indricotherium*. It lived 25 to 30 million years ago in the regions of Pakistan, Mongolia and China. It was twice as tall as an elephant, and weighed more than about ten modern rhinos!

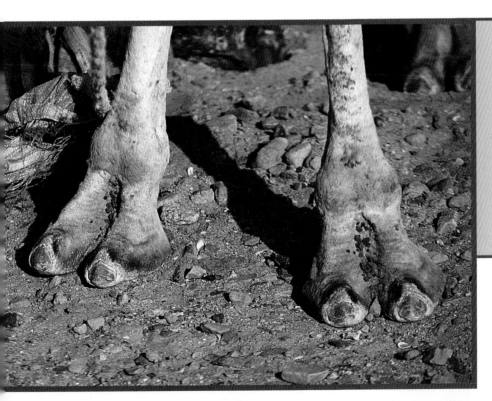

Camels walk on two large, hoofed toes, which have tough leathery pads underneath. When a camel puts its foot down the toes spread, to stop it sinking into the sand.

Scissor-toothed hunters

The word 'carnivore' means a meat-eating animal. Many animals are carnivores, but there is also an **order** of mammals known as Carnivores. It includes cats, dogs, wolves, foxes, bears, badgers and weasels. The feature that links all Carnivores is a pair of meat-slicing back teeth, called the carnassial teeth. Many Carnivores are meat-eaters, but some are omnivores and one (the giant panda) is a vegetarian!

Cat-like Carnivores

Cats, hyenas, mongooses and civets are all related Carnivore families. All of them have retractable claws (claws that can be drawn back in). Hyenas have huge back teeth specialized for crunching bones, while mongooses are small, agile hunters that sometimes live together in colonies (groups).

Cats themselves are superb hunters. They have strong jaw muscles for a lethal bite, and their meat-slicing teeth are razor-sharp. They have excellent eye sight and good hearing.

Many cats kill their prey with a bite to the back of the neck, using their canines – dagger-like teeth. However, big cats like this lion kill large prey by clamping their jaws into the front of the animal's throat and suffocating it.

Dog-like Carnivores

Wolves, foxes, bears, racoons and weasels are all dog-like Carnivores. Unlike cats, they cannot retract their claws.

Wolves, wild dogs and foxes are all part of the dog **family** itself. (The dogs we keep as pets are descended from wolves.) Like cats they are hunters, but they also eat other food. Dogs rely on their sensitive noses to find **prey**. They do not lie in wait, but chase their prey instead. Wolves and wild dogs hunt in packs, but foxes hunt alone.

The racoon family and the bear family of Carnivores are closely related. Many of them are omnivores. Bears are the biggest of all carnivores. Kodiak and polar bears can weigh up to 1000 kilograms (as much as a small car).

Weasels, stoats, badgers and otters are known as mustelids. Most of this varied family are **predators**. Weasels and stoats have long, flexible bodies for chasing small animals along burrows or hunting them in the water. Badgers are worm specialists, while wolverines are fierce predators that can kill reindeer.

*Giant pandas look like bears but are more closely related to racoons. They are vegetarians, living almost entirely on bamboo shoots. Pandas are found only in a few places in China. They are among the world's most **endangered** animals.*

Clever-fingered climbers

Lemurs, monkeys, apes and humans are all primates. Most live in hot parts of the world, particularly in forests. Many primates are tree-dwellers, but a few **species** such as baboons and humans live on the ground. Primates have excellent eyesight and a good sense of touch. Their hands are designed for grasping things, and most have flat nails rather than claws.

Similar bodies, different behaviour

Most primates have not become specialized for a particular lifestyle. Their hands and feet, for instance, are still similar to those of their early **ancestors**. Primates have **adapted** to the different places they live in by changing their behaviour, rather than by changing their bodies. So, although a human hand looks like that of a lemur, it is used for quite different activities.

To learn new ways of behaving and to remember them, you need to have a big brain. Primates generally have large, complicated brains.

The majority of primates spend their lives in trees. Smaller monkeys and lemurs, like this Verreaux's sifaka, run along branches on all fours and leap from one tree to the next. Gibbons, other apes and larger monkeys often swing from branch to branch instead.

Primate types

The biggest division within the primate **order** is between lemurs and their relatives and the monkeys and apes. Lemurs and related species such as bush babies have longer snouts than monkeys and apes, and wet noses, like dogs. Their eyes are usually large, because most of them are night-feeders, and their ears are large and moveable.

Monkeys have shorter faces than lemurs, dry noses and smaller ears. Most South American (New World) monkeys can feel and hold on to things with their tails, whereas monkeys from Africa and Asia (Old World) cannot do this.

Apes include gibbons, orang-utans, gorillas, chimpanzees and humans. They do not have tails and have broad chests.

Growing and learning

Young primates have a lot to learn before they can survive by themselves. As well as learning how to find food and avoid **predators**, they must learn how to fit in with their group. It takes two years for lemurs to become adults and ten years or more for gorillas, chimps and humans.

Most primates have only one baby at a time. The baby clings on to its mother's fur from soon after birth and depends on her for food and care.

Air-breathing swimmers

Some mammals have **adaptations** that allow them to live in water. The two biggest **orders** of sea mammals are the seals and walruses, and the whales and dolphins.

Flippered carnivores

Some scientists classify seals and walruses as Carnivores. Their **ancestors** are thought to have been rather like bears. But today they look very different from bears. They live in coastal seas, especially in cold polar areas, and their bodies have changed to suit their watery lifestyle.

Seals and walruses are streamlined, so they can move quickly through the water. Their ears are small or have disappeared, and they have a thick layer of blubber (fat) under their skin that keeps them warm. Their arms and legs have become broad, flat flippers. However, they are not completely adapted to water life. They need to breathe air, and they have their babies on land.

Like the Carnivores on land, seals and walruses eat meat. Seals eat fish, octopuses, crabs and shrimps. Leopard seals and sea lions eat penguins. Walruses mostly eat shellfish from the seabed.

*Up to a million walruses may gather together on a beach in the **breeding** season. Each walrus mother only has one pup. Pups grow quickly on their mother's extra-rich milk, and are ready to go to sea after a few weeks.*

Dolphins and other whales live in groups. They communicate with each other using a wide range of sounds and movements. Dolphins also use sound to find food, using an **echolocation** system similar to that of bats.

Whales and dolphins

Whales and dolphins spend their whole lives in water and cannot survive on land. They have no back legs, but have developed a tail like a fish. In fact, whales and dolphins look much more like fish than like mammals. But they still need to breathe air, and they feed their babies on milk.

Whales and dolphins can be divided into two groups: the baleen whales and the toothed whales. The largest whales, such as blue whales, fin whales, right whales and humpback whales, are baleen whales. They are named after the sheets of horny material (baleen), which they have instead of teeth. To feed, the whales either swim through the water with their mouths open or takes great gulps of the ocean. The water escapes, but food (shrimps or small fish) is caught on the baleen and stays in the whale's mouth.

Toothed whales include dolphins, porpoises, killer whales and sperm whales. They eat all kinds of sea creatures, from shrimps to seals. Killer whales sometimes eat other whales. Sperm whales feed on squid, which they catch from the ocean bottom. They can stay underwater for over two hours, and dive to depths of up to 1000 metres.

Sea giant

The blue whale is the largest animal that has ever lived. It can grow to 33 metres in length and weigh 135 tonnes.

Long-nosed giants

Elephants are unmistakable. With their long trunks, tusks and large ears, they are unlike any other animals. Elephants live mainly in grasslands or forests, and eat grass, leaves, tree bark and other plant food. Family groups of females and their young live together. The groups are led by the oldest female. Male elephants leave their family groups when they are about eight years old and live alone or in all-male groups.

Elephants have long lives – they may live to a ripe old age of 60 or 70. A baby elephant takes time to grow up. It drinks its mother's milk until it is 18 months old, and it is not fully grown until it is about 17 years old.

An elephant can eat up to 300 kilograms of food a day – that's the weight of twelve big sacks of potatoes! So finding enough food is a big task. Elephant groups keep on the move, travelling up to 45 kilometres each day. They often eat day and night, only resting during the middle of the day.

African or Asian?

There are only two **species** of elephant alive today – the African elephant and the Asian (Indian) elephant. African elephants are bigger than Asian ones, and have bigger ears. Their trunks also end in two 'fingers', whereas an Asian elephant has only one.

African elephants are the world's biggest living land animals. They weigh up to 7.5 tonnes – as much as a small truck.

Elephant trunks

An elephant's trunk is a nose, a hand, an arm, a hosepipe and a trumpet. The elephant can use it to smell the breeze, or sniff the ground for underground water. The end of the trunk is very sensitive, and can pick up objects as small as peanuts. But the trunk is very strong, and can carry heavy things like tree trunks. Elephants can suck up water or dust in their trunks, and spray it out to give themselves a shower or a dust bath. They also make noises through their trunk to communicate with each other.

Ivory teeth

An elephant's tusks are overgrown front teeth, which can grow metres long. Elephants use them to dig for water, to scrape bark from tree trunks, or to break down small trees. Males sometimes also use their tusks when they fight over a female. Elephants' tusks are made of ivory. Killing elephants for their ivory is no longer allowed, but poachers illegally kill thousands of elephants each year.

Asian elephants have been used as working animals for hundreds of years. They are still used today in parts of India, Burma and Thailand.

For eating, an elephant has only four huge molars (grinding teeth), two above and two below. Although they are very hard, they do slowly wear out. Once they are worn down, a new set of molars replaces them. Altogether an elephant has six sets of molars. When the sixth pair is worn out, the elephant can no longer eat properly, and eventually starves.

Is it a mammal?

We have seen that most mammals are hairy or furry, **warm-blooded**, have four limbs (arms or legs) and feed their young on milk. But some mammals have become so completely specialized for the life they lead that they don't seem like mammals at all!

Fishy mammals

Dolphins and other toothed whales look similar to some fish, especially sharks. Like sharks, dolphins have streamlined bodies, fins and a tail. Dolphins have up to 300 teeth, and sharks also have many teeth. Dolphins give birth to live babies, and some types of shark do too. These similarities are mostly due to the fact that both sharks and dolphins are ocean **predators**. They need to be able to move quickly through the water and catch their **prey**.

Certain differences between sharks and dolphins however make it clear that they belong to separate classes. Like all fish, sharks have gills and can get the oxygen they need from water, whereas dolphins have lungs and must breathe air. Sharks cannot keep their bodies warm in cold water, whereas a dolphin's body temperature stays much the same no matter how warm or cold the water is. Also shark babies have to fend for themselves once they are born, whereas dolphin mothers feed their young on milk from their **mammary glands**.

Sharks like this mako shark look similar to dolphins and porpoises. However, the shark's gill slits show that it gets its oxygen from water rather than breathing air.

Flying mammals

In a similar way, bats have some similarities to birds because both kinds of animal are **adapted** for flying. Both birds and bats have wings, and both are limited in how big they can grow, because they would become too heavy to fly. But birds have feathers and beaks, whereas bats have furry bodies and a mouth with teeth. Also birds lay eggs, while bats give birth to live young and feed them on milk.

Scaly mammals

Pangolins live in Africa and southern Asia. They have long noses, strong, clawed feet and the top of their bodies are covered in overlapping scales. They feed at night on ants and termites, which they dig out with their strong legs and lick up with a long tongue.

Because of their scales, you might think that pangolins are reptiles. But in fact they are mammals – they are warm-blooded, give birth to live young and feed their babies on milk. Their scales are actually made from hairs.

Glossary

adaptation change of a living thing over many years to fit into the place where it lives better

ancestor relative from long in the past. The ancestor of a group of living things is the species from which the group is descended.

breeding males and females producing young

cell tiny package of chemicals that has all the properties of life. All living things are made up of one or more cells. Most plants and animals are made up of millions of them.

class in classification, a large grouping of living things (e.g. mammals), smaller than a phylum but bigger than an order

digestion process by which an animal breaks down food so that it can be absorbed into the body

digestive system an animal's gut. It is the part of the body that digests food; it includes the stomach, intestine, and bowel.

echolocation a system that animals like bats use to 'see' using sound. They make high-pitched sounds, and build up a picture of their surroundings from the echoes that bounce back to them.

endangered in danger of becoming extinct (dying out altogether)

family in classification, a grouping of living things that is larger than a genus but smaller than an order

fossils remains of ancient living creatures found in rocks

genes genes are the way that all living things pass on their characteristics from one generation to the next

genus (plural **genera**) in classification, a grouping of living things that is larger than a species but smaller than a family

mammary glands milk-producing glands used to feed young on the belly or the chest of a female mammal

marsupial mammal whose young are born very tiny and undeveloped. For the first few weeks after birth marsupials live in a pouch on their mother's stomach.

migrate to move between different parts of the world

nocturnal active at night

nutrients chemicals from the digestion of food that nourish our bodies

order in classification, a grouping of living things that is larger than a family but smaller than a class

organ a part of the body that does a particular job

phylum (plural **phyla**) in classification, a grouping of living things that is bigger than an order but smaller than a kingdom

placental mammals mammals that give birth to well-developed young

predator animal that hunts other animals for food

prey animals that are hunted by other animals for food

species group of living things that are all similar and can reproduce together

warm-blooded animals that are able to keep their body temperature about the same, even when their surroundings are colder or hotter

Further resources

Books

Collins Field Guide: Mammals of Britain and Europe, David MacDonald and Priscilla Barrett (HarperCollins, 1993)
This book is a guide to identifying every species of mammal in Europe and in the seas around it.

Life Processes: Classification, Holly Wallace (Heinemann Library, 2000)
A guide to the most common mammals found in Britain.

Mammals, Jim Bruce (Kingfisher, 2001)

National Geographic Book of Mammals (National Geographic Society, 1998)
A good general reference book on mammals, with excellent photos.

The Wayland Book of Common British Mammals, Shirley Thompson (Hodder Wayland, 1998)
A guide to the most common mammals found in Britain.

Websites

www.AllAboutMammals.com/subjects/mammals/
www.cccoe.k12.ca.us/bats/default.html
www.natzoo.si.edu/Animals/animals.htm
www.nhm.ac.uk
www.mammalstrustuk.org/frameset_kids.html

Index